Three Blind Men and a Lady

I0447495

A heart-warming insight into an art therapy intern's initial journey counseling three blind men and a blind woman

By Lola Carlile, M.A., Ph.D.

Three Blind Men and a Lady

Three Blind Men and a Lady

A heart-warming insight into an art therapy intern's initial journey counseling three blind men and a blind woman

Lola Carlile, MA, Ph.D.

Masabi Press

Masabi Press
PO Box 2663
Salem, OR 97304
www.masabi.org

Copyright © 2012 by Lola Carlile. All rights reserved.

No part of this book may be reproduced, stored in a retrieval system, or transmitted by any means without the written permission of the author.

Printed by www.createspace.com 9/12/2012

ISBN 978-1479303625

This book is printed on acid-free paper.

Because of the dynamic nature of the Internet, any web addresses or links contained in this book may have changed since publication and may no longer be valid. The views expressed in this work are solely those of the author and do not necessarily reflect the views of the publisher, and the publisher hereby disclaims any responsibility for them.

Thanks

As always, I must thank my late mother who always supported my endeavors no matter what they were. I also wish to thank my sister, Evelyn Sieren Celli, for her amazing support and love.

Preface

After teaching all grade levels except second grade for more than thirty-eight years, I retired at the tender age of 58. But I was already on track to enter another career – that of an art therapist.

How did I ever arrive at that destination? Well, honestly, it was because of my students. I don't know how much my students learned academically, but I do know one thing – they were motivated and prepared to learn because of the classroom environment I provided.

As one university student said, "Your class is just like therapy." When probed about what she meant, she added, "You incorporate the arts into your lessons and they are, uh, just, well, therapeutic. I love coming to your class." Mrs. C. took notice.

And so the saga of art therapy school began. I had to take a full year of art classes, since I had never taken an art class either in high school or college. As a matter of fact, my mother could not understand, for the life of her, why in the world I wanted to be an art therapist.

"We don't do art. No one in our family is an artist. I just don't get it."

Later on, Mother would get it as I tried to show her things that art therapy worked for.... I sat down with her and said, "Here's a pencil and some paper. Draw!"

"Girl, you know I can't draw!"

To which I responded that the art did not have to be anything beautiful – it could just be scribble for all I cared. And then she started.

She gripped the pencil so hard I thought she might break it and with her top lip and teeth covering the bottom of her jaw, she began to draw concentric circles and the speed with which she drew increased. She looked like the energizer bunny in action.

And that's when she got it – we talked about how she never lets go of things (boy, I can remember that from my interactions with her, especially if she was upset about something) and how she never seems to stop.

I remember my mother working late into the night cleaning house, when she would wash ceilings, floors, and so on. Our house was immaculate.

Mom got it. And she was so proud of me. For that, I dedicate this book to her. Thanks, Mom, for giving me the background to respect and value education. I am here because of you. God bless you!

 It took me three more years to go through the program and this book chronicles one of my groups during my practicum. The group consisted of four individuals who were diagnosed with varying types of schizophrenia, in addition to their blindness. I use the term blind, since all four told me to use that term. They said they did not like being called visually-challenged. All four were over the age of fifty and I can say, without a doubt, working with them was one of the most enriching experiences of my life. I do miss them so!

The following chapters are random takes at working with this group. I held at least six other groups each week (not including individual sessions, so this was a small part of my practicum experience, but one that touched my heart the most).

Read on and check out one of my first lessons as I get ready for the experience of a lifetime….

Journal

Chapter One

Why did I promise them to make pizza? Can't we just do some art?

"The best and most beautiful things in the world cannot be seen or even touched. They must be felt with the heart."
Helen Keller

So what is the point of writing all this down? Tomorrow is the day I said we would make pizza. I bribed the group. I did. I told them we would make pizza if they would just please take the homemade clay and make a fake pizza. *What?* For art. *Do what?* You heard me. To make art. *Why?* So I can say I did art with you. So I don't have to have a culinary art therapy group or whatever they might dare call it…. Please?

And that day is tomorrow. How can I make this a memorable session when all they want is to eat? The process is so important! The process! Remember it. Revel in it. Don't try to just get it done. Enjoy the moment. How can I impart those words and feelings to my three guys who are blind? And my very opinionated African-American woman who used to see, but then someone threw something caustic at her. Seems like she said it was her stepfather. Has been blind ever since….

Can I even dream of making it an artistic moment?

Challenge them with facts. Challenge them with the history of pizza. I frantically look up several articles about the colorful history of pizza; I copy one such story and I enlarge the font on the paper. Why? They can't read it. I must read it to them. Will they enjoy the story or should I have rewritten it in more interesting language? No, I don't have time. The stolen copy from the net will have to work.

But just read and make the dough? That's all? What will they remember? They must know what the ingredients are, but none of them know Braille. They don't like to read. They all say it almost in unison. Two are early blind (born blind) and the other one became blind after an awfully traumatic accident twenty years ago. He knows. He remembers.

So the ingredients are laid out in big black letters that they cannot read. But I am not giving up. I need to surface those bolded black letters that are almost one inch big each. I need to make the surface readable for them. So they will be proud they can remember and share with their housemates exactly how one makes this pizza. . . .

YEAST
SUGAR
WATER   =
FLOUR
OIL
SALT

Is making pizza art?

Glue… glitter… what should I put on the letters to raise them up so my guys can proclaim the names of the ingredients? Wait, my mind is working overtime. Why not put these same labels on the bottles and jars themselves? Then I can ask **THEM** to go get them. Am I being innovative or am I about to insult my clients? And here I am just beginning. I am still an intern.

D-Day 12 hours away. . . .

Pizza

Ingredients

- 1 package (.25 ounce) active dry yeast
- 1 teaspoon white sugar
- 1 cup warm water (110°F/45°C)
- 2-1/2 cups flour
- 2 tablespoons olive oil
- 1 teaspoon salt

Directions

1. Preheat oven to 450°F (230°C).
2. In a medium bowl, dissolve yeast and sugar in warm water.
3. Let stand until creamy, about 10 minutes.
4. Stir in flour, salt, and oil.
5. Beat until smooth.
6. Let rest for 5 minutes.
7. Turn dough out onto a lightly floured surface and pat or roll into a round.
8. Transfer crust to a lightly greased pizza pan or baker's peel dusted with cornmeal.
9. Spread with desired toppings and bake in preheated oven for 15 to 20 minutes, or until golden brown.
10. Let baked pizza cool for 5 minutes before serving.

"The beautiful and the good are identical but the fleeting impressions created by the work of a cook or a musician disperse even as they are being experienced. Raphael's painting 'The Transfiguration' is immortal, but Carême's 'Ragout de truffes à la parisienne' lasts while it is being eaten, just as roses that last as long as their fragrance can be enjoyed."

Lucien Tendret (1825-1896)
French lawyer, great-nephew of Brillat-Savarin.

Chapter Two

Am I teaching culinary arts instead of practicing art therapy???

"Cooking is one of the oldest arts and one which has rendered us the most important service in civic life."

Jean-Anthelme Brillat-Savarin

Is Lola here? I bet she is going to get the ingredients for our pizza. Yeah, that's what she is doing! Lola, are you here?

The sound of DJ attempting to find out if I was to keep my promise was alive, loud, and a bit annoying. How dare he think I would make a promise and not keep it? I learned that lesson many years ago when I was teaching. You don't promise kids something and not follow through. You are toast if you do. So, DJ, I am telling you, I will not promise you something and not do it. I promise. DJ is actually not that annoying. He pulls at my heartstrings at times.

They called me retard. I'm not retarded. I didn't like it when they called me retard. DJ is as solemn as a priest blessing a casket. And I cringe within. How many times have I heard people call out RE-TARD? Laughing and shouting and putting each other down. And now I hear how it feels from the other side. The one being called RETARD. Why do names hurt so much? As I gaze at this fifty-something man who is as innocent as a five-year-old, I think of what it feels like to be called names. Skinny! Chicken legs! Those names resonate even decades later. **Him** retarded? Why would anyone call him that? He is kind and genuine and tries oh-so-hard.

How can I make this art therapy session meaningful for him? If I bribe him with food, he is all for doing anything I ask him. Color? Sure. Change colors? Sure. And it means nothing to him other than his institutionalized mannerisms. To get along in the big house one must be positive and do what is asked of one. No one is here to hurt you, DJ. You can say you don't like doing art. I won't take it personally. I am trained to depersonalize what you say. I am here to help you. It doesn't matter about me at all.

Relax, DJ, and know that you are a marvelous creation of God and that I respect you and will only think of what is good for you as I prepare for our group sessions. You like the pizza. I can see it dribbling down your cheek. You liked even more hearing about the history of pizza – can you imagine it was a treat for low-class people and then the King and his girlfriend decided it was wonderful? And pizza became good fare for everyone. You listened, DJ. I saw you. You smiled as I read the story. I hope you enjoyed it immensely. Sleep tight, DJ. Think of the pizza and all the love at our table.

Okay, so we are all going to use clay. All of you shake heads emphatically NO! Oh, oh. I thought this would be a cinch. So they can't draw and paint, but they surely can manipulate clay. But they hate it. *Nope. Can't stand it. Don't like to touch it.* I look at Reese. He is a high-functioning, depressed early-blind gentleman. He says it how he feels. He doesn't pull any punches. He won't say he likes something and then turn around and stick his finger down his throat when you're not looking. Nope, Reese is an honest Abe.

This place isn't exactly intellectually challenging, he shares with me one day. That goes right through my heart. Oh, dear one, *I* will challenge you with facts and figures and statements that will make your hair stand straight up! So, with your recent pizza experience, how was that? Did *I* challenge you enough?

What is this talk of what *I* am doing? Am I forgetting that this is not about me? I am not here to succeed or fail – I am here to help guide my clients, not think of myself. Down, ego, down! Get out of here. I need to work without you today and tomorrow. You are just part of me, but a part I don't need to address or be reminded of much. Go away!

Ah, better….

So Reese loves the pizza. He wants to put the cheese on the top. He gently lets the shards of mozzarella cheese dribble out of his fingers and onto the waiting dough and tomato spread. *Did I get any on the table? Did I do okay? Man, this smells good.* No, no cheese was wasted for this pizza. You did a great job! I wonder: if this man had been trained from little on up to be literate, would he have had a more enjoyable life?

He is depressed with psychotic features. What does that mean? He did tell me that he was suicidal at times, but not

lately. Whew. I don't know how I would handle that. I would be so worried. I couldn't let him go home. But there again is that elusive **I.** It is not up to me. It is not up to me to do anything but provide him with an hour of socialization and healing, as art, no matter how you describe it, is healing.

I ordered a blind stylus-and-clipboard sort of thing. You put the thin plastic sheet in the top and then write on the film. The rubber underneath (on the clipboard) allows the film to have raised lines. Reese smiles. Yeah, he's used that before and didn't like it. He said he had to write backwards. Huh? Uh, I used it and didn't have to write backwards. Wouldn't it be nice if the guys had an idea of what images are? The two, RJ and Reese, are early-blind. They have no concept of images, of dark and light, nor of a tree that a child can draw....

I draw one on the film. I gently pull their fingers over the ground, the trunk, and the foliage. They say they can feel it. They seem cautious. Just how much time should I dwell on this or where should I go with this....? I'm an art therapist. Keep it on the art. The process. And where exactly do we begin?

Chapter Three

How am I to assess a totally blind man with visual cues? Am I on the wrong track?

"The only thing worse than being blind is having sight but no vision."

Helen Keller

I am mesmerized by my three guys and lady. They are all so very different. I want to help them, although I only have five more months essentially in which to do so. What can we accomplish that will make a difference in their lives? I am committed to converting the traditional assessments to ones that will correlate with the early blind.

I know nothing about Braille, other than it's a regulated system of raised dots. So why can't I create a system of raised something-or-other for art? Well, something like that does exist, but that's not what I am talking about. I am talking about creating something the guys can touch and then create a picture to reflect their cognitive understandings.

Okay, most art therapists know about the Silver Drawing Tests. How about the one for conservation? The one with the glasses? The client is supposed to draw in sequence what a full glass will look like in seven stages from full to empty. How can the guys show they understand that?

I've wracked my brain and I go back to when I taught primary grades. We used felt boards. Why couldn't we create a felt series of "glasses" that would have varying levels of "liquid?" Sounds like it might work. So, I pull out an old board and glue on a piece of felt. Step #1 complete.

Now, the question for validity…. Is this a valid reconstruction of that measure? They aren't drawing, but they are completing the concept just the same. I can't wait to try it this Friday. Should I use the same thicknesses for all the pieces or should the liquid be made from a heavier format? Also, should I make them larger or the same size? Would that make a difference? I think I will try doing both and see what the guys do. Can't wait until Friday….

Yes, I know these are grown men and they have dignity. But they also want to learn and if I can help them help others, I believe they 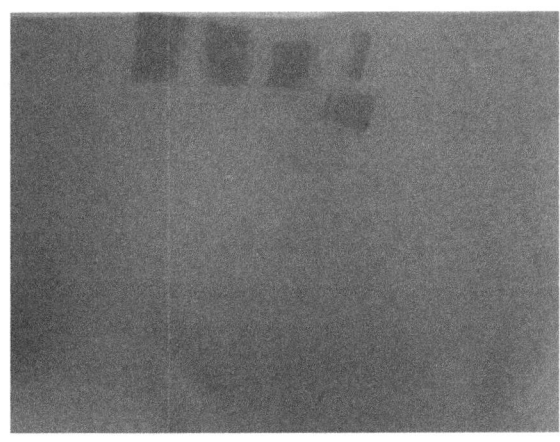 will be extremely happy. But back to those felt boards. Look at this one. Get the idea?

They will be able to put the glasses with partially filled contents in order on a felt board. Looks like what I came up with is a cheap rendition of a task, but it works. DJ enjoyed the "test." He was able to figure out all the sizes, except for the last two. He could not distinguish which of the last two was bigger. No matter how I asked him. *Nope, that's pretty much it. They are the same size.*

I remain incredulous, knowing that the working of the mind still mystifies me sometimes. Yes, I have information on DJ now, but I'm wondering what to do with it. Obviously, he can determine size, but then can he? How will I use that information in the coming months?

Chapter Four

I don't even know what they know! Early blindness is not synonymous with unintelligent. But what do I have to go on? How do I assess them?

To be blind is not miserable; not to be able to bear blindness, that is miserable.

John Milton

Our group lost a member today and gained another. Hopefully, Reese will be back soon, but Carla has joined us for the time being. I was able to observe her during music therapy yesterday and she loves music. She was hopping in her chair and shaking the maracas and shouting, *Oh, yeah! Uh huh! Oh yeah!*

Her enthusiasm invigorated even the sleepiest of the twenty-some clients using their instruments of choice: castanets, drums, tambourines, and more. The leader, a young tender-hearted man about thirty, played the djembe with his entire being.

I couldn't help but tap my feet as the music wafted through the rafters. A good time was had by all. I thought Carla would make a great addition today to our group, since Reese is talkative, but the other two gents… one repeats things over and over and only hears himself, it seems, and the other says nothing other than, *Yeah,* or *I'm good.* Carla would be a good mix for them, I hoped.

Not sure why Reese isn't here. I sort of miss him and I know that I am not supposed to get "attached" to my clients, but I'm just human. I am humbled that I have been given the opportunity to work with this unique group among my six weekly groups and assortment of individuals I see for art therapy.

So as they begin to enter the *art space*, as we call it, DJ is already talking in his radio announcer voice, *I don't want to do clay. I hate clay.* Gently, I say, *I just want to find out what images you can make sense of.*

I do not have a clue and if you bear with me today, perhaps I can make some sense of what we are doing. I don't say this out loud, but think it intensely. What am I doing? For one hour a week, are they getting anything or are they just tolerating me? It's about them. It's about the process. Why don't I trust the process with them yet?

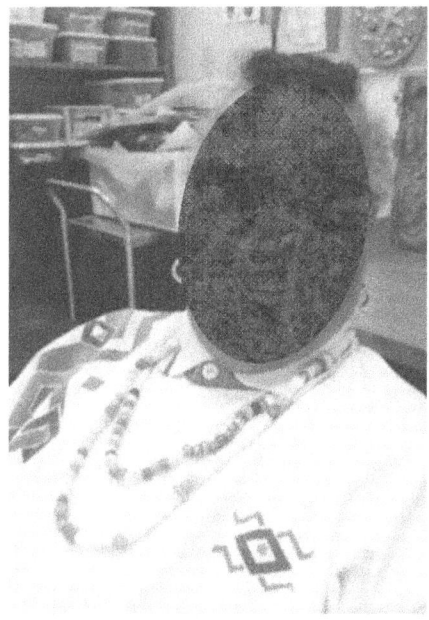

Well, if ah cain't go on the outing, then I wanna make beads. Where are mah beads? I cringe. It's Carla ready to explode if she can't string beads. But that's not what I was planning this week, Carla. I need to find out what you remember before when you were sighted. I need to find out what the others know. So, I gather my wits and say something to the effect that I want to make this group learn more things and I need to find out exactly what they are able to do.

*Well, okay. But I still wanna string mah beads. But, okay....*DJ is silent, thank God. He is not complaining at all and Ron is quiet as usual. Three blind individuals and I want to test them all, but what do I do with them while I test individually? Can they write their names? No. None of them.

What do you do when you sign something? Make an X? Silence. I know they can hear, but they are not listening to me. Where are they? Their bodies sit in front of me at the round table. Their faces are here but their minds are somewhere else. I have to think quickly.

Then, out of the blue, RJ remembers his Nevelson piece and shouts out, *Hey, can I paint my sculpture?* By this time I really am ready to hand him paint and just let him do it. I am ashamed immediately that I am caving in and have no firm feel for where we are going today. So I inform them all that I need to do some assessments and after that each one is welcome to work on their choice. Carla shouts *Beads! I wanna make beads.* Great! You can make beads. I am happy to give you clay.

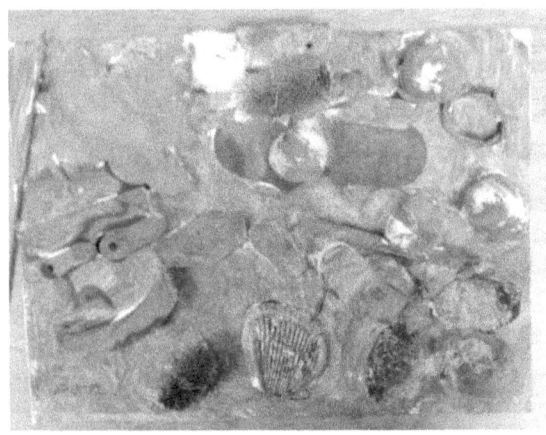

And, sweet quiet Ron sits there ruminating and rocking back and forth. While I ask them to hold the pencil in front of them and draw a circle, square, triangle, and rectangle the best way they can, I sigh with relief. They are all scribbling one shape or the other. I have some felt pieces and ask each one to identify the shapes. They are all able to do it. Another deep, deep sigh.

And then all hell breaks out – actually, it's not hell, but I am so tired it feels hot in here and I peel off my sweater. I search for a paint shirt for DJ and find his sculpture. But as I gaze at him I realize he has pretty dressy clothes on. What if he gets acrylic paint all over him? Nah, it's poster paint for him. I ask him if he has any desired color and he says, *It don't make any difference to me.* Again in that loud, radio announcer voice. I ask if black is okay. Why do I care either? The black ends up being turquoise and neither DJ nor I care. He is happy as a clam. *Just remember that when you are not on the newspaper, you are not painting your sculpture!* He smiles and says *I know. I like this. I really like this.*

Well, actually that's not the way it happened entirely. While I was searching for paint and helping DJ put on his paint shirt, I was handing Carla a paper plate of red clay. Red clay that stains and gets all over you. Red clay that needs to be washed from your hands and she sits there and just rolls out beads. One bead at a time. I give her more clay.

Don't worry about the holes – I'll make them this time. Just relax and make those beads. I almost thought *damned beads.* But that wouldn't be truthful. It's late at night as I write this and now I am thinking *damned beads* because I got to sit around for about thirty minutes putting holes in about fifty clay, soft, staining beads. But Carla was happy.

Ah love art! Oh, thank you! This was fun. Do ah get to paint them? When will they be ready? Can I use different colors? Will you show me?

And what is Ron doing? He is not the squeaky wheel. He sits there wringing his hands. I have given him clay as well. He doesn't complain. I'm not sure he even cares what he does. He makes two rock-sized balls. *Do you want these? Do you really care, Ron?*

I give them to Carla. Let her make more beads. It's been an hour and time for them to leave. I need to figure out how to get them to clean up after themselves. I am just happy they were content and occupied in the process. Time later on for learning new things. Are they exhausted as I am?

I reflect on something Ron told me once in a session. When asked what would be something they really wanted (holiday gift giving), he said, *I just want to see again.*

Tears puddle in my eyes as I wonder what the heck I am doing here. I always panic when I over-think things. I need to just let the art process work. It does in regular groups. Even with my Muslim deaf/mute gentleman who gladly makes snowmen, and decorates trees and gingerbread men. These blind clients create a vacuum in my head. I am sucked dry and can't think today.

Chapter Five

Why over-plan? Can't we just do the same thing as the others? Why does it have to be over-planned? Or am I just lazy?

Every time I learn something new it pushes some old stuff out of my brain.

Homer Simpson

Instead of trying to figure out some clever and ambitious way to have my blind folks do art, I decided to let the art show me. So, during my morning session with sighted clients, I showed pictures of MLK, Jr. and told about his life in five sentences or less. We discussed what freedom meant to each of us and the artwork displayed was what I expected. Much the same. Flags. Birds. And then the pm group.... same plan, same directive – different folks.

So, what do you all know about Martin Luther King, Jr.? A plethora of information was forthcoming. More than most of the clients before even dreamed of knowing. Reese was absent as he is not feeling well. How we miss him. He would have liked today's session....

Ron says little. *Okay. Yeah. No. Good.* On to the next person, Carla, who is a black woman (she does not wish to be called African-American) and she says, *Hell, no, I am not free!* And then she begins a diatribe about her abusive and horrible father. *He even tried to run over my sister with a John Deere tractor. See this scar on my lip? He pushed me into a nail. He was so horrible. Lordy, I am not free from him and he is dead.*

Powerful moments and humbling ones at the same time. I'm a novice. What do I do? I tell her that it seems she hasn't dealt with this lately. *Hell, no, I haven't! I haven't told a soul!* Again, my antennae are raised. I must share this with my supervisor. Thankfully, Carla provides a segue to what we will be doing next. She says – and this was not scripted, I swear – *I want to draw some and that will make me lose this anger.* I sigh. I look at the others and they are silent. Are they listening or off in their own worlds again? I don't know.

A few moments elapse and we prepare to use markers and large sheets of paper (24 x 20) to draw anything we want. I explain to them that each marker is a different color and they can use just one or they can change when they want to show their moods change. They all nod and I surmise they understand.

Carla begins drawing some small marks. *Is that a 1?* I say yes and her face radiates with the biggest smile I've ever seen on her. She continues in this fashion with 2 through 5. I fib a bit, but I know how important it is for her to realize she can remember things and do them. She continues drawing her hands, a mirror, a sun, moon, stars, and is very happy with the session. She titles her page FREEDOM FROM THE PAST. When she leaves the session, she says she feels *just great!* Art was the miracle worker, if a miracle indeed occurred.

DJ is taking his time, rhythmically drawing gentle, large strokes of color in purple. After about ten strokes, he changes to another color in another place on his paper. He chooses green, purple, black, and brown. He titles his page FREEDOM – OH FREEDOM! He smiles, grunts, and says it's been a great session. He says he would have shared what freedom is like for him, but he's *afraid my ex-stepmother will come and get me.* To do what no one is sure, but he laughs and says he *can't say a word.* Secrets. Past dungeons. No one knows.

Ron has taken the marker and drawn horizontal spirals. He changes markers each time. The spirals are colorful and remind me of slinkies. We talk about slinkies. Only Carla does not remember them. Was this a guy thing? Ron is asked what to title his piece and he says, *I don't know*. I say, "Oh, you want to title this I DON'T KNOW?" He laughs loudly. I haven't seen him laugh this way before. *NO!* Well, what do you want to title it? He is quiet. I am quiet. Everyone is quiet. What did we say it reminded us of? *Uh, slinky. Yeah, let's call it SLINKY.* He says he feels good. I tell him that next week we will expand his vocabulary and he'll have to find some adjectives to use besides *okay, good,* and *yeah.*

Today both my clients and I have found freedom. I have found freedom to trust the art – to know that it will do its thing and its curative qualities are best found when one does not push or artificially create undue stress. Just relax and allow it to flow.

I am so humbled by their sincere efforts I forget to take out my camera phone and snap what they are doing. I am getting over the fact that their art does not have to be aesthetically pleasing to me or to anyone. It is what it is. It is their art and their movement and their humanity flooding the paper. I hope I am worthy to work with these folks.

Chapter Six

Am I a teacher or a therapist? Can't I be both?

The real difficulty, the difficulty which has baffled the sages of all times, is rather this: how can we make our teaching so potent in the emotional life of man, that its influence should withstand the pressure of the elemental psychic forces in the individual?

Einstein

For the first time in months all four clients are ready for art. The question is, am I ready for them? I search my soul and try to make this art experience as nonthreatening as possible. But it's a lot of work for me. I languish and brood before they arrive. I wonder if I need to reinvent the wheel. That seems backwards to me, but I don't really know what to do. They are adamant against working with any kind of "clay-like" media. Okay, we did do it with the cookies. But we can't be cooking all the time. This is not culinary arts, but art. And my supervisor says we have ants….

Okay, I begin with them. Does anyone remember why we were off on Monday? DJ offers his take on it and begins with his loud and droning voice, *Yes, it was Martin Luther King, Jr.'s birthday.* And I return with, and does anyone know why we celebrate his birthday? Silence and then again DJ's voice, *Freedom. Yep, that's it. Freedom. We are free. I am free. You are free.*

The others patiently sit there awaiting some epiphany to come to them. Even when DJ mentions freedom, the others sit there with a flat affect. I am not sure I can tell if they are even awake at the moment. So we just sit a bit and let it sink in. That's something I have learned in my art therapy program – I need to be okay with silence. I don't have to fill it with chit chat.

For the moment I am not sure what to do, though. I have prepared materials for them to begin making a puppet, due to the fact that my supervisor asked me if I had done puppets with this group and I took that as a significant moment in that I should do it… I'm always second-guessing people. Maybe I should ask him what he would like me to do with them. After all, he is a seasoned art therapist and I am just a newbie. A neophyte. A beginner. Sorry, folks. Everyone has to begin somewhere. I guess I wouldn't want to be the surgeon's first heart patient in surgery, but someone has to be the first....

I digress. So I talk to them about making a puppet, to which Reese says acutely, *What's the purpose of that?* Uh, good question, I think. Um, so that we can have new experiences of creating with paper mache. *Uh, will we get dirty? Is it messy? Will it come out of our clothes? I don't like messy. I don't know if I want to do that....* DJ is obsessing now about making puppets and the other three still sit there like statues. I am glad Reese has rejoined the group, but at the same time, he makes me think really hard. He is not out to flim-flam the teacher, no sir, he is himself and he usually is disgusted with ordinary. And I am just that – ordinary!

Deep breath. Another deep breath and one more for good measure. Let's just try it, folks, okay? If you absolutely don't like doing it, it will be over and you won't have to make another one. But in the case you might like it, well, that's a cool thing and you'll be proud of your masterpiece.

Another deep breath. Okay, here are the toilet-paper rolls. We have to make a head out of newspaper and tape it to the TP roll. Laughter. Snickering. Yeah, we are using toilet paper rolls. They are clean and have never been used. More laughter. More snickering.

This work is harder with the blind because I have to talk more. In working with others, I can demonstrate without using a lot of words, but I have to use words to explain what

I am doing. I am already tired and it's just 2:15. Fifteen minutes and it seems like an eternity.

I have to use the restroom now! shouts DJ. He has never done this, but I know he means it. I jump up and ask if he'd like for me to guide him there, to which he is ever more appreciative. He can guide himself back since he won't be in power mode....

Back at the art station, the other three continue to sit in silence. This is going to be a long session. DJ returns and loudly announces this return. No one says a word. I'm ready. Let's just plunge in. So, now I will give you a TP roll taped to a square of cardboard. Your job is to take your newspaper piece and make a ball out of it. When it is the size you want, you can take the masking tape and put tape all around it. Yeah, masking tape is really easy to use and tear. You wouldn't want duct tape. *Oh, no, we wouldn't,* comments DJ again. *It's very difficult to use and can peel off your skin.* Hum, I wonder. When did he use duct tape and why? That's another story, I presume....

They cooperatively engage in making the puppet's head and glue it onto the toilet paper roll. We are now ready to use the paper mache. This is easy stuff. I precut the newspaper and all they have to do is dip the strips into starch in the metal bowl and put it back on the head.

Easy for sighted individuals. But what about those who don't even know the location of things. So I tell them *on your left is a metal bowl with bleach in it.... **BLEACH?** roars DJ in dismay. Why are we using bleach?* I put my head down and sigh. I meant to say starch. Muffled laughter. Yeah, they are paying attention, huh?

A few minutes later, the heads are beginning to be filled with paper and by the end of the session two clients have actually finished their entire head. Two have just finished more than 60% of the head. Hooray! It worked. They did it. Halleluiah. How was it? Did you like it? *It's okay. Yeah. It was good. I would never do it again. But it was okay.*

Another day. Another session. And they actually did something. It was so quiet….did they actually benefit from it? I'm not sure I know. But I feel they spent the past sixty minutes in their heads learning something. Even learning they didn't like something, but learning something and not having to dwell on getting somewhere alone. We were together. We were…

It didn't matter that they could not see what color their puppets were. They pasted and glued and felt the heads form. They laughed and imagined a finished product. And we all celebrated.

Will their puppets look this good? They don't care about color or style… or do they? Next week I'll ask them what kind of a puppet they want to paint and what color they would like. Would they like their puppet to look like them? Or do they just want to be wild? Who knows what the future may bring…?

Chapter Seven

Am I a genius or ridiculously under some illusion that I can teach color to blind people who have never seen color? Even more so, why? Is it important to them or should it be?

There are not more than five primary colors (blue, yellow, red, white, and black), yet in combination they produce more hues than can ever been seen.

What are we gonna do today? It's DJ and his voice is loud and everyone in the center can hear him. It's not quite time for our group session. I am hiding out in my nook, with a portable divider separating me from the community. I am sitting there trying to figure out what I am doing with his group today. And he shouts out again, *Hey, LO-LA! What are we gonna do today?*

Too lazy to get off my duff and quietly go out to where DJ is and tell him in an inside voice, I shout out, "I don't know. I'm thinking…." And I wonder why he does this every Friday and every Friday I answer the same way….

He is good natured and says, *OK.* And I wonder why or what I should be doing. Should I have gotten up from my nice warm chair and opened the temporary barrier and walked over to him and answered and then returned to my nook? Or, should I have just pretended I wasn't even there? I digress with these questions and thoughts. Some days I am frozen to the spot and just sit there and wonder about it all. And other days I am busy as a beaver creating his first dam.

My room divider is my dam. And I tear it down and it isn't even significant most of the time. Since it is visual, it's psychological. The seeing population get it, but DJ has no idea it is there. He believes I am in close proximity and should be able to have a conversation with him, albeit quite a loud one.

In the background I can hear Carla's voice, *Ah wanna make beads.* One of the staff members gently reminds her that art therapy begins in about thirty minutes. The staff member is sweet and young and has no clue what I am going to do with the group, although she does say something about not having time to do beads at that moment. Satisfied, Carla returns to drinking her cup of coffee.

I'm quiet and I'm here and I don't want to be rude to you, Carla, but I gotta think. I gotta be quiet so my brain will work. Otherwise, our session will really suck, 'cause right now I don't have an idea. I planned something, but it isn't even important or fun for me, so why would I make you do it? Please just drink your coffee and keep DJ occupied. Can't you talk to him about something?

Something in my head says that color is important to our world, so why not teach some semblance of color to these folks? I know that blue is a cool color. How can we determine what that looks like to the blind? I know that a long time ago, or maybe in a dream I had, blind people would meet you not with a handshake, but would touch you and get to know you that way. DJ has told me that they don't teach the blind to do that anyway. Imagine meeting someone and they are feeling you up all over the place? Creepy! Well, not really, but the hand became a pivotal part of my thought process.

That's it. They will trace their hands. No, I will trace their hands. I will cut it out. Then I look around in the varied boxes of realia – kinesthetic stuff. Stuff they can touch. Stuff with dimension to it and I find two bags of glass. Seriously – shards of glass, but they are not sharp. They are meant for crafts. They are cool to the touch. Voila! An idea is born. They can glue these down. How? They will have glue all over. No, they can just place the shards down and I will hot glue 'em down. I'm ready. It's time. I get up and remove the dam, uh, barrier, and announce it is time for the group.

DJ is steady on his feet and his brand new cane akin to a wizard's wand is unfolded and he makes his way to the back. Carla and Ron cannot make it there without assistance. If I time this right, I will have ten minutes shaved off their hour just by accompanying each one at a time to the art nook.

Ready, Ron? Here's my arm. We're going straight and to the right. Okay, and around DJ and here is your chair. You got it? Carla, I'm coming…. Beads? No, not today. We're going to learn something new.

Thank you, chile! I love you, you know? I love you! Carla's face is radiant. I want to hug her and say I love her, too. I want to take her on trips. I want her to enjoy life. She said the other day that she was tired of sleeping alone. DJ said she asked him to marry her. He doesn't want to because he doesn't want her sister managing his money. He likes being single. My heart beats rapidly. I'm tired. This is a difficult and challenging group for me because I am in this blind as well.

Don't you all know I don't know what I'm doing? I'm running on intuition, experience with life, but no experience with the blind at all? I love you and want to help. But sometimes I feel so inadequate….

Hey, LO-LA! Are we gonna make cookies? It's DJ and then Carla joins in, *Ah wanna make beads.* How am I gonna create a stress-free environment for them today? A meaningful one?

Oh, wait, I forgot to look for Reese. There he is. Patiently awaiting me to accompany him to the art nook.

Everyone is seated. I take a deep breath. They are such good human beings. Sitting there quietly waiting for me to do my thing. Whatever that is.

Okay, today we are going to work on understanding what colors are – and blue is our first color. Have you heard any sayings that use the word blue in them?

Yeah, "he's blue today." Great, DJ. Sometimes I get tired of your chatter, but today you are really reaching out and helping the group understand. Great! Thanks!

Yes, that's right. Blue is a mood. A feeling. A sad mood. Blue is a cool color. Like you've heard people say – "He hasn't been himself today. He's been sort of cool to me."

You kin say that again, chile! Boy, blue is a sad color. It's the color for me when I don't get to make beads! Girl, laugh! You know ah am kiddin'! Seriously, I love you, Carla! You have so much gusto. So much life. Yes, you are right! And I really like your humor today, Carla! It's infectious.

Reese then adds, *I guess that's what the blues are all about....* Only Rod sits there saying nothing, mouthing nothing, just sitting. Is he blue, I wonder?

I give each person a white sheet of heavy poster board. I ask each one and make the circle, drawing his or her hand on the paper. I quickly cut them out and give each person a blue marker to color their hand. DJ draws with glee, getting a lot of the marker on the table. I don't cringe. I believe, albeit mistakenly, that it will wash off easily. We still have vestiges of blue on that table…

Carla tries to outline her hand in blue and Reese manages to color most of it. Rod just makes a few marks and says he's done. Judging by the look on his face, I think he is done. Again I wonder what is going on? This man was sighted until he experienced a terrible self-inflicted wound on himself in his thirties. That means he was sighted far longer than he has been blind. Is he sad? Angry? He just sits and says *Okay. Fine. Yeah.*

Now, to divvy up the glass particles. We talk about the feel and texture of them. They are so cool to the touch and I remind the group that blue is cool. It is a serious color, but it can also be soothing, like the ocean, like the sky. It can be relaxing. It is not a negative color. Just cool.

It's time to leave and I have thirty minutes in which to glue all those shards down and I want to make sure I do justice to my group. Yes, they are my group. I want to say my friends – my people. But they don't belong to me. They are on loan from the Almighty for a few months. Just a few months….

Chapter Eight

*So it worked once. Am I ready to try it again this week with **RED**? Will it get old? Or will they really learn something?*

An optimist is a person who sees a green light everywhere, while a pessimist sees only the red stoplight.... The truly wise person is colorblind.

Albert Schweitzer

Why are we humans so interminably stubborn? We had something good going on and now I am going to beat it into the bush. *Let's do more,* my freed brain screams. *Let's learn about all the colors. Yes, we can do it.* **That's booooorriiinnngggg....**

No, you will learn the differences in color and someday down the line you will be thankful you know the difference. Carla is asking for beads again. No! We are going to learn about red. What words do you hear in our language that use red as a descriptor?

Red as a beet!
   Red, red rose....
      Red faced
There we go! Red. Scarlet. Hot. Like fire. Like when someone slaps you on the face or spanks you – that fire lit from within is a red color....

By now this group is learning to placate me. I wonder if their hands drawn and cut out by me will teach them the color red. I carefully cut out a hand shaped out of felt. It's warm. They all smile as they attempt to glue it down to their cardboard hand. And they ask if they can put fire in the hand.

My heart skips a beat and I realize that this may somehow be just a bit meaningful to them. What could we use? We need something that will stand up and proclaim its very redness....

And out of the corner of my eye I spy some tissue paper and give each a sheet. Each individual begins to place the by now crumpled red tissue paper amongst the red felt hands. Red. They got it, by George, they got it!

Then DJ bursts my bubble. He says as loud as ever, *I hope we aren't going to be doing more of this next week. I don't think I will attend if we do.*

Bummer. But the others don't join in his protest and he smiles and says that if that is my job to have them do the art this way, he will just swallow his regrets and cooperate.

DJ, you do have a way about you. Why is it that they say you are developmentally delayed? You are naïve. But you are way honest and a joy to have in group. I want to hug you, but my professional training and distancing mantra says not to. If you could see me, you would see my warm smile and admiration for you....

We talk about last week and the blue hand covered with cool stones that are blue. We talk about the way the colors are represented in our speech. And DJ shouts out, *Yes, just like I was blue a minute ago, but I am fine now. I am fine.*

The lump in my throat will soon dissipate, but using art therapy or what I hope is art therapy with this group is very challenging, yet oh so rewarding at the same time.

We talk about the warmth of the red felt and each one pets the hand as if it were a dear friend. Red is not only warm, it is hot and as if on queue, Carla shouts out, *Wahl, I thank that a fire engine must be red. Seems I remember something about a red fire engine. It went real fast and was painted red. That makes red a hot color, too.* She then giggled and said, *Ah needs to wear some more red, cuz I am one hot girl!*

Giggles emanated from our cubicle and one of the staff members came back to make sure I was still there. Surely, this group couldn't be having that much fun doing art, or could they?

The rapport maintained by the very different and unique men added to the fun ingested by our newest member, Carla.

In my heart I was thinking, I bet you would look cute in a nice red dress. I don't know why people don't color coordinate for you. I know you can't see the color of your clothes, but if you could, I don't think you would dress the way you do. Your sister should do something about your clothing.

And that's when I looked about and saw how ragged and unkempt the entire group looked and wondered if it mattered at all. Just as long as they were clean. But that's another matter, 'cause they weren't.

Chapter Nine

Clay beads at last! I'm running out of ideas and they sound easy enough.

Everything has its beauty, but not everyone sees it.'
　　　　Confucius

I've heard Carla's mantra for several months now, *Ah want to make some beads.* And I've just put her off until now and now is the time for us to rise up, make our clay, and roll those beads.

When the group comes back to the circular table and each individual is seated, I ask them to guess what we are going to make today.

Reese sardonically replies, *How would we know what you have in mind? We haven't been able to ascertain what you think.* And then with a little giggle, he adds, *Or if you think!* Carla hoots and the other two simply sit stationary unaware that a joke has been made.

I begin to explain that we need to make our own clay, as we do not have a kiln at the center, so we need clay that dries by itself. I know there are commercial clays, but those were nixed in the beginning by the guys and I don't want to remind them of that negativity. So, I say, "Are you ready to make some clay?" I am enthused. Reese is a bit enthused. Carla is ecstatic and the other two mumble something to the effect that it's okay.

Not having a faucet nearby, I tell the clients I have water in the middle of the table. Each person will be using a half cup water, 1 cup salt and 2 cups flour. They will mix this together and add water until they have a nice elastic dough. This is harder than one might think.

Working with a spoon is out. That was apparent when Ron threw the bits of flour and salt every which way.

Why don't we just use our hands to mix the clay? It's okay if we get dirty, let's just know that we can all wash our hands at the end. And, if you put it in your mouth, well, it's gonna taste pretty darn nasty.

DJ adds, *Well, I wouldn't eat clay. That would be stupid. Who would be that stupid?*

I groan. Because I have had sighted individuals in this very center try to eat the homemade clay. Right there at this table. Right in front of me.

As the mixing begins, Ron says, *I'm done.* He has a mess, nothing is mixed and he's done. Is art helping him at all? Would anything help him? There are times when I wonder how an individual such as Ron can exist. He demonstrates very little emotion and says everything is okay. There has to be a feeling, caring man inside. He does come out eventually, but not today.

I inspect each bowl and give advice as to whether they need more flour or water. After about twenty-five minutes of mixing, talking, and sharing, most of the clay is ready to roll.

Step #2 is defining how to roll something. This should be easy but it is not. Don rolls a long snake-like piece and DJ just makes a blob. Only Carla is sailing along, humming, shaking and making those beads.

Well, of course, one must put holes in them before they dry or they aren't beads. Carla has pointed that out to me. I knew that. I was gonna tell you all. I was just waiting for the right time. The time has come: please take the pencil that is in front of you and push it through one of your beads. Pull it out and, voila! When it dries, you will be able to thread something through it.

I'm thinking yarn or wire. Or string. Not sure which.

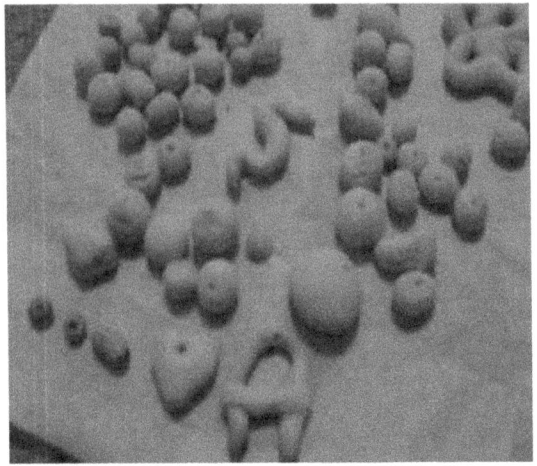

Carla has done a good job of making a variety of beads. She has added some letter shapes and hearts to the bunch. She is ready to set them out to dry.

Ah wants to paint 'em now. I calmly ask her to feel them and see why they aren't ready. They need to be hardened so we can paint them. Next week they will be ready.

The other three are getting up and ready to go back to the main room. I mention there is a bit of clean up, even though it would be far easier for me to clean the mess up than them.

But I want them to have satisfaction and I want to practice my patience. A win-win situation for all.

Chapter Ten

Okay, maybe they've forgotten all about the red and blue hands. Can we make white hands today, please?

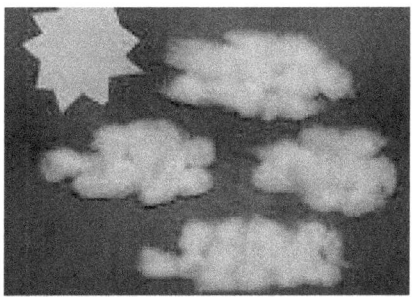

No problem can be solved by the same consciousness that created it. We need to see the world anew.

Albert Einstein

I'll make it easy for ya'll today. I'll precut the hands so you won't have to spend ten minutes holding your hands out while I trace them. Yep, I have those images of your hands when we did red and blue! But shhhh, I won't mention that….

I hand each individual a cotton ball. Touch it… what does it feel like? Then I tell them that all humans have this color in their eyes – it's white. Clouds are soft and very light – yes, they are white.

We talk about the word white. What have they heard that is white? Wedding dresses. Correct. *White as a ghost.* Yeah! More… *the white sand on the beach.* Yes! White does not really have a temperature. It is. It is the ultimate light.

They are smiling now as I tell them they can glue cotton balls over their hand cut-out. They quietly do so. I don't even hear talk about beads. Yes, they need to paint their beads, but I've forgotten about them. And to tell the truth, only Carla was interested in making them and/or painting them.

Next time – or when she finishes – I'll tell her to paint her beads. She can decide on the colors. When she was a prebuscent child someone threw acid in her face and she was immediately blinded. But she remembers. She remembers the attack. She remembers colors. And now she can smile….

I tell them that most pillows are white. They are fluffy and clean smelling. White is that color. Carla says, *Yeah, I remembah when my sheets were all clean and smelling like bleach. Ah likt that smell.*

The men shake their heads and DJ says *I like to smell my sheets after they have been washed. I wonder if they are white, too?*

Dare I even try the color green next? We could have a wonderful time with that color…Better not push my luck. Red, blue, and white….

Chapter Eleven

Mistakes can turn out really great! To wit, this frame reminiscent of the beach….

Creativity is allowing yourself to make mistakes. Art is knowing which ones to keep.
          Scott Adams

It had been a long week. I had paint left over on many plates for clients who didn't attend group for one reason or another. I was tired and hadn't really prepared anything for my blind group. That was usually the one group I had to have plans for since they were my special group. I had very little (to be honest, NO) experience working with the blind and doing art. I had some preconceived ideas, but no real in-the-trenches experience. So, I worried all morning about what to do with them that particular afternoon. Little did I realize that anything we did was fun and challenging for them. Even just sitting around telling stories – we had fun most of the time. I don't know why the worry factor always nudged me, but I worried all day on Fridays until the group was over and then wondered why.

So, here we had enough plates to give each of these clients one plate. I told them to use a brush and to just swirl the paint around. They had a grand time doing so, with Carla singing *Amen* at the top of her lungs as she painted away. The curvature and strength of the plates allowed them to spend more than a few minutes mixing and mashing the paint about.

As I sat there and watched, I applauded my genius, and then was hit by DJ and his good-sense repertoire of one-liners, *Hey, Lola, I think I painted the table some.*

Sure enough, the paint was all over the table and some of it found itself right on Mr. DJ's hands. It didn't matter. The stuff was not acrylic, or was it? I had to think back and immediately gave him some sturdy wet paper towels and told him he could wipe his hands and I'd get the table.

Of course, you are right! I could have prepared better by putting newspapers on the table before allowing the paint to be mixed and spread. But I didn't. I allowed myself to breathe and realize we will all make mistakes. And mistakes are to be learned from....

I gave each person an opportunity to use the hair dryer and dry the paint so we could move on to the next phase and that was to place beads, shells, etc. on the plate. When the group finished, I hot-glued the pieces exactly where the individual had laid them. Voila! Some beautiful pieces were indeed made.

We had no choice of colors, as the colors were the leftovers from other groups.

Just look at what you can do! Just relax and go with the flow. Carla's was the most beautiful. But they all were pleased with the results the next week when they came in and "felt" and "saw" their art. These were keepers and most of them took them home to put in their rooms.

The encounter with the shells garnered many a discussion about the beach. DJ added his *I love the beach* and *I am going to go there next month in the summer.*

Reece nodded and said *I love the smell of the beach. This piece really does not smell.* And then Carla injected, *We should make it smell. What could we do?*

Yuk. I thought of opening a tuna fish can – I hate the smell of fish, so nixed that idea quickly before it came out.

I probed and we talked about ways to make our beach plate come alive. Maybe we could spray something on it? But what?

We never figured it out, but certainly had a good time just talking about the beach and what was pleasurable about it.

I should have brought in my Ocean CD, but ideas come late to me at times....

Chapter 12

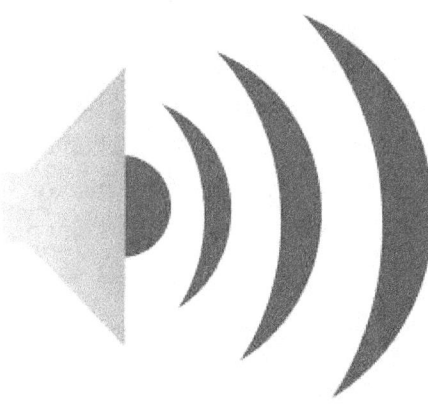

Sounds? Somewhere I heard that the blind have amplified hearing…am I on to something?

A blind man can make art if what is in his mind can be passed to another mind in some tangible form.

Sol LeWitt

I am not sure where I got this idea, but today I wanted everyone to revel in art making. I know that the folks in this group like coming to meet with me. Sometimes just to talk. Not always to do. So we can talk, right? My time is almost up with my internship. I stifle a sob as I realize I will not be visiting and working with these individuals soon. And I will miss them. More than I know.

So, today we will work with a material I think you all know about – aluminum foil. They used to call it tin foil.

Did you know that tin foil was used for the first audio recording in the US? I hope that is of interest to you. I am trying to expand your horizons and entertain you…where did that word come from? Seeping out from under my educator background? No, this is NOT about me. This is all about you all….

There are different thicknesses of aluminum foil. We have a medium thin piece to work with today.

What? We're gonna work with it? What we gonna do?

Good question! I don't care what you do with it. You can crunch it up. Hear that? I'm crunching my piece. Here, you can each have a piece. Crunch it up! Yeah, that's good. Some of you are rolling it into a ball. You can fold it, expand it, tear it. Have fun.

We spend the next few minutes laughing and tearing, pulling, and making a general noise of having fun….

So, are we done now? I pause and ask them if they want to have bigger sheets. They can form it to any shape they want.

Yeah, that's cool.

Give me more.

Whoa! That feels like ice to me. DJ is rolling his hand on the shiny side of the foil. Carla says she likes how cool it feels. What color is it?

Silver. Silver. Cool.

Time to leave. They have enjoyed the shapes and are comparing the sizes of each one. They pass them around. Ideas. Feelings. Texture. Smooth.

Well done, my friends, well done!

Chapter Thirteen

Why don't we use some yarn and weave or something like that?

In Old Europe and Ancient Crete, women were respected for their roles in the discovery of agriculture and for inventing the arts of weaving and pottery making.

   Carol P. Christ

I guess I was too naïve thinking the folks would be able to braid three pieces of yarn. My first mistake was that the yarn itself is very thin. Close your eyes and feel a strand of ordinary yarn. Not too easy. Now take another strand and yet another and try braiding them with your eyes still closed. Enough of frustration 101!

So, when I got into the mood to really work with yarn, I opted to use two strands. The group was excited to start something new.

Gimme that there yarn, I can make some braids. Yep, I done made 'em when I was younger, but they weren't this thin. I mean, my hair wasn't this thin....

The lone female in the group is excited enough to pay attention to the task at hand. The guys are sitting there with bland, expressionless faces, being respectful enough not to gag right there at the table. Well, I 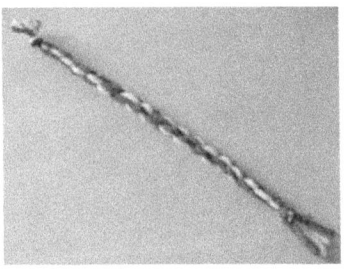 have thought this through and I go through my spiel about weaving and how many men were weavers (was I even sure of that comment?) and that if we got it down really well, we could, well, we could make lots of stuff.

As if they care.

I retrace my thinking and decide that I will make some braids and they can braid the thicker braids. Maybe next time I should use strips of cloth or, better yet, strips of felt. That would make it easier to feel. That might even look pretty nice....

I ask each member to tell me a color s/he would like to use. I have a choice of red, blue, white, and black. All of the men choose red and blue. Carla is different. She wants black and white. She remembers colors and she likes the stark contrast.

They sit patiently moving one piece of yarn over the other and then remembering to pull the under piece up and over. Repetition. Repetition. Small sighs emanate from those who are getting it.

DJ comments, *Ya know, I am wondering why we are doing this* (as if I hadn't thought of that by now). *What are we going to do with these?*

Good question, I think. Out loud I say, "Well, we can glue them to our collage we started the other day. It will give it some texture. They look really nice when you roll them up.

I almost get hit on the head as I stare at Ron. He has balled up both pieces and tossed them in my direction. Is that a grin sort of that is plastering his face? I see what he thinks of this activity. But even to get some feedback from him is wonderful. At least he is able to let me know in some silent manner what he is thinking.

I am tempted to throw it back at him. The ball is only one or two inches thick, so it won't hurt anyone. Does professionalism enter into my mind? With this group a lot of things go on that might not seem as professional as I would like, but they seem happy and say the hour goes by way too fast. No, I keep the ball and tell Ron, "Pretty good aim there!

You hit me on the noggin." To which the entire group laughs out loud. Yes, it has been a good day again. A good day. Award-winning project, no. But a project that

was useful and therapeutic.

Later on I get a pretty good idea of having the folks decide on a shape and for me to use glue to draw that shape on a square of burlap. Then they can use a large (pointless, harmless) threaded needle (threaded with yarn) to go in and out on the glue bumps. I haven't tried that with them, but I think it might be fun, especially as they get used to using yarn some more.

I just found some new glue ideas- try using glue dots! The folks can lay them down and then place flowers or other realia right on top of them! Try making decorated hats and/or caps.

These are easier and far safer for folks to handle.

Chapter Fourteen

As I think about this group, I wonder how they ever got to be so unlucky – it's difficult enough to be blind, but to have a mental illness on top of that?

It would seem that our actions have lucky or unlucky stars to which they owe a great part of the blame or praise which is given them.

François de la Rochefoucauld

Triskaidekaphobia – unlucky 13 – so that's why I am writing a fourteenth chapter. One might wonder why I thought that this matters. This phenomenon is actually considered a phobia (so named in 1910) and is part of DJ's fears. He doesn't like to think of the devil, being spooked by evil, and doesn't want to cross fate any more than need be. So, in honor of DG and the group, I am not tempting fate more than I need to do so.

Seriously, I am not really phobic about things. But in this case, I want to make sure I cover all my bases. It's just like that repost request you get or "send this email to five of your best buds." I can't stop wondering if what the heck – I'll just do it in case!

While I started this journal out as a way to understand what I was going through and how to check for my progress with this group, others have asked me to share with them my experience since it is also a novel experience for many beginning art therapists.

 Whether you work with the blind, developmentally delayed, or other challenged individuals, the most important concept to embrace is caring. The empathic therapist will figure out what to do, even if it's not strictly in line with the art process – maybe it'll be oral art – as in stories.

The next chapter will entertain you as you go through a session with the folks on one day when they were not going to touch a thing – not for art's sake, not for my sake, and certainly not for anyone else. They just did not want to do anything but talk and talk we did…. Although I panicked at first and worried I was doing something wrong, I continued with our talking and it turned out to be one of the most honest and fulfilling sessions ever.

Chapter Fifteen

Honestly, I am so scared I
am not doing my job! Today
the group simply does not
want to do anything but
talk. They have already
informed me in a very
polite, but direct manner,
"Let's just talk today!"

If you don't know the trees you may be lost in the forest, but
if you don't know the stories you may be lost in life.
        Siberian Elder

I am known generally to think outside the box and my former life as an English teacher helped immensely as this session continued.

Ya know that I am tired and I don't want to do anything, but I do like to talk. Lola, can we just talk today? This coming from Reese who had been out sick for a few weeks. Not just sick! He was in the hospital very ill. So, looking at the others, I simply asked what they thought.

Ah likes stories, Lola! Tell us a story! added Carla, but then I saw the light in DJ's eyes and asked him what he thought.

I think I'd like to tell a story about the group. Like sort of make it up! I like this group. It might be fun.

Then laughter from all of them. Yes, this had to be about them. And so, how would I start? I liked DJ's desire to unite the group. So what do we wanna do?

Wahl, I wanna get away from here.

Yeah, me, too! I wanna go to the beach.

Lola take us there!

So I began writing as quickly as I could, reading to them as I did so:

One day Reese, Carla, DJ and Don decided they did not want to have group. They wanted to get away, so they…

They stole Bob's car! Yeah, they took it away. He could come with them, but he's the director. He can't leave the others alone, but we stole his car (laughter, laughter)….

And so they asked Lola to find Bob's car. It was a ….

Big limousine –

No! It was a hot rod.

It was a cool black car big enough for all of us to fit in….

…late model black sedan. The group got in and started the car. Lola was driving.

And then?

Oh, Bob heard them and came running out after them. He chased them down the street. He made it to their car when they were stopped at a red light. He jumped onto the car!

Yeah, he was so mad. But we were having fun. We wanted to go to the beach….

As they stopped at a red light, the director, Bob, came running up to the car. Lola revved up the engine *(much laughter here)* and started to take off. Bob jumped on top of the car!

Oh, let's say that we tied Bob onto the car. We don't want him getting hurt and we certainly don't want him stopping us…

The story went on for four full pages. The group was laughing and snorting and I'd never seen them so animated. Finally at the end of the story, the group became folk heroes who were allowed to share their story. Bob was not mad. Lola was not fired. All's well that ends well. But the next time the group met, they were thrilled that I had made copies for them even though they could not read it. Plans were in the making to tape it, but, sadly, that did not occur. It did not take away from the marvel of writing together.

Looking at the story therapeutically, I could see a longing for all of them to escape the normal routine; not only to escape it, but to move to a level of independence, choice, etc.

Although they were practical about matters (they couldn't drive and I would have to), they dictated a wish to do something fun that they described. Going to the beach was a way to do this.

The themes of enjoyment, fulfillment, comraderie, as well as choice was evident in their story. Had I thought of it then, perhaps the next session would have been more useful if they had been able to touch starfish, clams, and shells and then to create their own ocean artifacts with clay or other regalia. Sometimes these ideas come too late to me, hence the importance of a journal so that I can remember and add to it as I bond with other groups.

Afterword

I hate the end. I hated it when school ended. Even as a teacher, I hated the last day of school. I bonded with my students and here I had to let them go. Same for my groups – 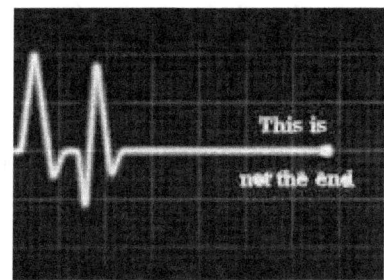 they would never be gone from my mind and my soul. I think of them frequently.

Why can't we get all the people together in the world that we really like and then just stay together? I guess that wouldn't work. Someone would leave. Someone always leaves. Then we would have to say good-bye. I hate good-byes. I know what I need. I need more hellos.

Charles M. Schulz

I knew the goodbyes would be sad. I knew I didn't want to leave, but it was time for the new graduate to move out into the world and begin a new career. As I met with the group, I told them I had really enjoyed working with them and that they taught me a lot. Their comments were bittersweet, with Ron saying, *Yeah, thanks, Lola.* And that was unprompted!

Girl, ah love you so much! God bless and keep you, was Carla's goodbye to me and DJ added *Even though I don't like art much, you tried hard to make me like it and I think I might like it someday. Just not now.*

Bittersweet, but from the heart. It hurt so much that I was not able to tell Reese goodbye, for he was back in the hospital and all we could do was offer prayers and good intentions.

I wonder if the next intern or practicum student will love them as much as I, or am I confusing love for bonding, empathy, and caring? Surely, she or he will find this group challenging, but sensitive and patient as well.

There's not a week that goes by that I don't think of these folks. There's not a week that goes by that I don't say a little prayer for them and hope that their life is filled with tender escapes and happy moments. And I go on. To them I dedicate this book and hope that all their moments are filled with love and pleasure. The appendices are filled with information that may help those of you who are working with blind or visually-challenged individuals. Remember to respect them enough to use the terminology they prefer. It is not up to us to create those labels.

Resources

Appendix One

Art Beyond Sight – A Resource Guide to Art, Creativity, and Visual Impairment

Art Education for the Blind, Inc.
589 Broadway
New York NY 20012
www.artseducation.info
AFB Press
American Foundation for the Blind
11 Penn Plaza, Suite 300
New York, NY 10001
www.afb.org

The amazing part of this book is that there are pages you may duplicate for educational purposes. The prologue by John M. Kennedy states, "…provides an avenue for the comprehensive exploration of pictorial art by the blind. This should be the right of the blind as much as the sighted. The hand is as adroit with pictures as the eye. Surely it was to be given its proper, full education. In recent decades research in psychology ahs shown that blind people have a strong native ability to understand raised representation. AEB has been taking note of this finding and offers this publication...."

The chapters include why one should teach art to people who are blind; theory and research of touch vs. vision; learning tools, which include verbal description, sound and drama, tactile diagrams, art making, and art in a broader context.

For a novice such as myself, the chapter by a graduate student who is blind and majoring in fine arts was amazing to me. She shares a time when she took life drawing and was encouraged to get up and sit near the model, frequently feeling her and drawing. Although she says it was a little embarrassing at first, the end of the day she was pleased with her work and thought nothing of it the next time she drew. She adds that she did not have a chance to do a life drawing of a male model!

Amazing is all I can say!

While the book was over $100., it was filled with incredible information I savored. Although it was poorly bound and fell apart the first time I opened it, I kept it rather than return it for another one.

The most salient information I gleaned from this book was the samples of tactile diagrams which are actual diagrams using a silkscreen method. Many art museums are incorporating this so that pictures can be redefined for the visually challenged or blind individual.

Teresita Fernández - Epic (Wall Meteor), 2009. Natural and machined graphite stones, tools, projection slides, 150 x 686 x 1 inches.
Courtesy the artist and Lehmann Maupin Gallery, NYC.

Blind landscape in museum.

Teresita Fernández - Portrait Blind Landscape, 2008.
Courtesy the artist and Lehmann Maupin Gallery, NYC.

Teresita Fernandez, artist.

For more information on this innovative and creative art, check out http://www.artknowledgenews.com/2009-10-31-23-34-12-blanton-museum-hosts-a-survey-of-new-and-recent-work-by-teresita-fernandez.html.

Appendix Two

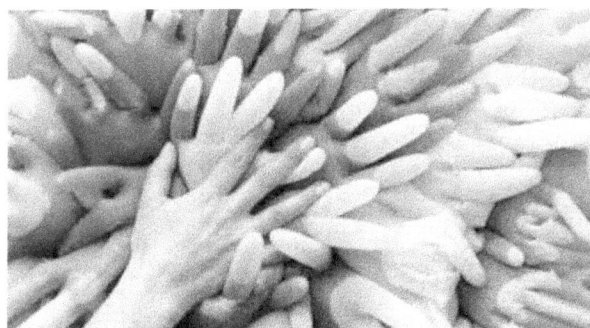

Websites, articles, and other information that might prove helpful to you:

http://www.artbeyondsight.org/teach/how-blind-draw.shtml#
an amazing individual who gives information on how to teach perspective, etc. to blind individuals.

http://www.artbeyondsight.org/handbook/az-museum-school.shtml
how to prepare your museum for blind individuals

http://www.blindwithcameraschool.org/adaptive-tech/
using cameras with the blind!

http://www.sc.edu/scatp/artQ.htm
activities and ideas in a blog format

http://www.tactilebooks.org/making/telling-touch.pdf
telling stories through touch

http://www.squidoo.com/museum-touch-tours-for-blind-visually-impaired
museum guides to blind

http://www.squidoo.com/museum-touch-tours-for-blind-visually-impaired#module91366201
how to prepare circuses, museums, etc. for blind individuals

http://www.squidoo.com/museum-touch-tours-for-blind-visually-impaired#module114930151
theater touch tours

http://www.squidoo.com/healing-gardens
healing garden instructions

http://www.healinglandscapes.org/healthcare-gardens/a.html
even just a small terrarium or sand try with cactus can be healing

http://nfb.org/images/nfb/publications/fr/fr28/3/fr280307.htm
materials and resources for use by blind individuals in classrooms

http://www.listeningislearning.org/background_what-is-description.html
http://descriptionkey.org/
an amazing service that describes videos so that the individual can "see" in his/her mind. The DCMP provides free access to thousands of captioned and described educational videos to registered members who work with K–12 students with vision or hearing loss.

http://iconline.ipleiria.pt/bitstream/10400.8/431/1/Sound%20Painting.pdf
sound paintings

http://www.blindcanadians.ca/publications/cbm/2/art-lesson-plans-blind-children
art lessons for blind children

http://www.ehow.com/list_6895303_art-programs-blind.html
art programs for the blind

http://www.blindartistssociety.com/
an online resource and support group for blind artists

http://www.behance.net/gallery/Origami-for-the-Blind/408386
Origami for the blind

http://www.flickr.com/photos/cobra_11/6809035716/
A blind man's amazing origami

http://www.foodiggity.com/burgers-for-the-blind-braille-buns-created-with-sesame-seeds/
Burgers for the blind

http://www.youtube.com/watch?v=x6E1z_KV2gs
A blind artist's story

http://www.ehow.com/list_6895303_art-programs-blind.html
Art programs for the blind

http://www.blindartgallery.com/article1.htm
Art education for the blind

Art

Directives

Appendix Three

Ideas that came too late, but might inspire others to use…

Some of them can be modified and others used as is. Enjoy! And these are not just for the blind!

Water Art

Materials: Heavy rough board, such as watercolor paper (the thicker the better); large-grained salt, eye dropper

Method: Fill the dropper with water, release as many or as few drops onto the paper as you like. Sprinkle with large grains of salt. Allow to dry. Feel the raised water spots! Can use cornmeal instead of salt.

Terrarium

Materials: Small green plants, marbles, stones, dirt, container, whimsical artifacts

Method: Explore a large terrarium or one that has been set up as an example. Discuss why terrariums are healing. Add dirt to container and place other materials in it. Water slightly and enjoy!

Making Paper

Materials: Wooden frame, sieve with holes of about 1 mm (available in a hardware store), Formica sheets, rectangular bowl/container large enough to fit the frame, mortar with pestle, jug, hairdryer, newspaper, green and dried grass (optional), flowers (optional), flat sponge, water

Method: Soak some of the newspaper in water (it's better if you let it to set for a day or two). Squeeze out the excess water. With the mortar and pestle, crush a little bit of paper at a time until you get a homogeneous paste consisting of fibers isolated from each other. Repeat this until you have enough paste. Fill the bowl halfway with water. Put the paper paste in the bowl and stir it to separate the fibers. Remove any resulting clumps. Immerse the frame in the watery suspension in the bowl. Slowly remove the frame from the suspension keeping it steadily horizontal. Eventually move the frame to even out the layer of fibers. Wait for the water to drain. Place a sheet of Formica on top of the layer of extracted fiber and squeeze out the excess water, without putting too much force on the sieve. Gently, remove the sheet of Formica and with it the sheet of paper, which will again be soaked with water. Dry the sheet with a hairdryer.
http://www.funsci.com/fun3_en/paper/paper.htm

Make a Bouncing Polymer Ball

Materials: Borax (found in the laundry section of the store) , cornstarch (found in the baking section of the store), white glue, warm water, measuring spoons, spoon or craft stick to stir the mixture, two small plastic cups or other containers for mixing, marking pen, watch with a second hand, metric ruler, zip-lock plastic baggie.

Method: Label one cup 'Borax Solution' and the other cup 'Ball Mixture'. Pour 2 tablespoons warm water and 1/2 teaspoon borax powder into the cup labeled 'Borax Solution'. Stir the mixture to dissolve the borax. Add food coloring, if desired. Pour 1 tablespoon of glue into the cup labeled 'Ball Mixture'. Add 1/2 teaspoon of the borax solution you just made and 1 tablespoon of cornstarch. **Do not stir.** Allow the ingredients to interact on their own for 10-15 seconds and then stir them together to fully mix. Once the mixture becomes impossible to stir, take it out of the cup and start molding the ball with your hands. The ball will start out sticky and messy, but will solidify as you knead it. Once the ball is less sticky, go ahead and bounce it! You can store your plastic ball in a sealed ziploc bag when you are finished playing with it.
http://chemistry.about.com/od/demonstrationsexperiments/ss/bounceball_2.htm

Embroidery

Materials: burlap squares (8x8); large plastic needles, yarn, glue.

Method: For practice, simply glue several dots on a sheet of paper. Instruct clients to feel the dried glue. Tell them they will make an embroidered piece using the raised dots as clues as to where to put the needle and yarn. When they seem comfortable with that, bring out several squares of burlap. Depending on your group, you can pre-glue simple shapes. Show them how to thread the needle (by touch) and then insert the needle right next to the first glue spot and up under the next one until all the glue dots are covered with yarn.

Sculpting with Sculpey

Materials: Sculpey – clay purchased from Michael's or online, very large needle, paper plate.

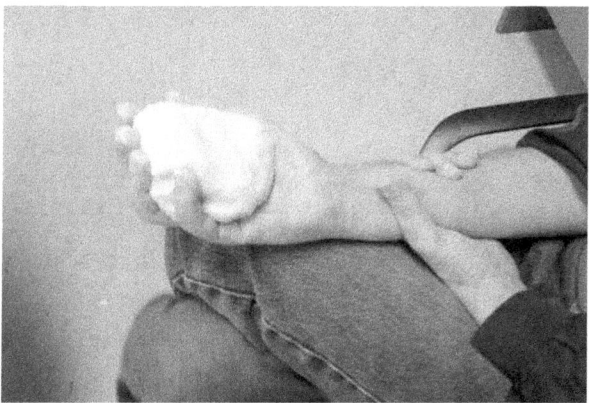

Method: Sculpey is very malleable and can be used to make beads. After rolling a few, use the large needle to make a hole. These will air dry, but it is still best to bake them at 250 degrees for at least 10 minutes. Cool off, thread them and you have a necklace!

Make Your Own Clay

http://www.dragonsaretooseldom.com/craft_clay.html
A great site for coffee clay (might be interesting for scent?),
traditional clay, molding clay, and sawdust clay (another
interesting one for smell).

Materials *for Coffee Clay:* 2 c flour, 1/2 c salt, 1/8 c instant
coffee, 3/4 c warm water.

Method: Dissolve coffee in water. In a separate bowl, mix
salt and flour, making a hole in the middle. Pour in half the
coffee. Mix until soft dough forms. Pour more until it
becomes consistency of clay. Create! Bake finished product
@ 250 degrees for an hour.

Felt/Construction Paper Villages

Materials: 11 x 17 white poster board, sand or glitter (preferably pink), one each construction paper: purple, pink, brown, black; white glue; scissors;, copy of "The Fortune Tellers," a picture book about Cameroon.

Method: Read the story. Share views about the beautiful landscape. Have each person cut out purple and pink mountains that would go completely across the page and glue them almost to the top of the poster board. Meeting the mountains will be the ground – glue some brown on the board. Create huts and trees in black and glue them on wherever you wish. Place the glue above the mountains and drizzle sand or glitter to create a scene at dusk.

Nevelson Sculpture

Materials: 1 11 x 17 light plywood or large heavy poster board, 0000 sandpaper, found objects (small pieces of wood, leather, cotton, seeds, etc.), glue gun, paint (optional).

Method: Lightly sand the board so it does not have any rough edges. Place objects lightly in any fashion. When they

are as desired, hot glue them in place. You may paint them with tempera paints, if you so desire. For a permanent look, use acrylics. Google **Louise Nevelson** to give a background to the clients about the type of sculptures she created. The result is a tactically rewarding piece.

Styrofoam Collage

Materials: Peanut Styrofoam pieces, larger pieces Styrofoam, white glue, either a light plywood sheet about 11 x 17" or a heavy poster board.

Method: Place pieces as desired. Don't glue them down until they are aesthetically pleasing! Use glue to glue them down. If desired, paint, using tempera or acrylic paints. I am very careful with the visually handicapped folks using acrylics!

Sand Tray

Materials: One of either: wooden or cardboard box with sides 3 to 4 inches high. (The wooden box is a craft clients can make the week before.) Enough sand to fill the form; found materials; optional water/plastic or glass containers.

Method: Fill the container with sand. Gently smooth it and place found materials in a pleasing manner. This is an interchangeable activity that can be rearranged daily or weekly. Ask clients to tell about the arrangement. Record their responses. Purchase a small rake to allow for changing scenes. Suggested found materials: rocks, shells, cactus, etc.

Rubber Band Magic

Materials: large rubber bands, marble.

Method: Start the rubber band ball by simply wrapping a single rubber band around a small marble until the band is tightly stuck around the marble. Keep wrapping rubber bands around and around till there is no give on it, and it's  tightly wrapped. Before you put each new rubber band on the ball, toss it up in the air with a little spin (it doesn't matter what direction).

Puffy Paint

Materials: Equal parts shaving cream, white glue, bowl, stirring spatula.

Method: Mix ingredients in bowl. When thoroughly mixed, use as finger paint or paint with a brush. When dried, the mixture remains puffy. Can divide into several small containers and add food coloring, but not necessary.

<u>Corks Ahoy!</u>

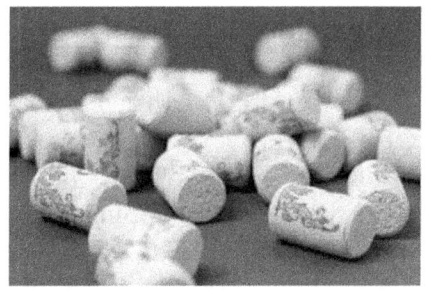

Materials: At least 20 corks, an 8 x 10" piece of thick cardboard or thin plywood. Be sure to sand the plywood so the clients don't get splinters OR have them sand it with 0000 sandpaper; glue, glue gun, optional paints, 12" rope.

Method: Prep the plywood or cardboard and place the corks in any fashion desired. Glue down when they are just right! Paint, if desired. Glue the rope to hang the piece.

Popsicle Sticks Sculpture

Materials: 100+ popsicle sticks, glue, optional paint.

Method: Explain that clients will be using only popsicle sticks to create something. Brainstorm things that might be made with them. Allow clients to use as many or as few sticks as they need. Discuss what their creation is at the end of the session.

Rock/Stone Collage

Materials: Bag in which to hold collected rocks, glue, thin plywood sheet any size, optional paints.

Method: Take a walk outside. Find an area with rocks/stones and encourage clients to pick them up, feel them, and keep

the ones they wish. Encourage them to use smaller ones, unless they wish to have a larger one as the base upon which the others can be laid. Pour water over them and feel the difference!

Leaf Relief

Materials: various found leaves or cut out ones from construction paper, crayons, heavy cardboard or poster board, any shape.

Method: This is a good activity to go outside and find leaves. If in an area where this is not possible for any of many reasons, bring in leaves for the clients to hold and touch. Have them place them down on the poster board and lightly use the flat side of the crayon, color around the leaf. Fresh leaves are a must! When the page is filled, clients can feel where the piece is smooth and the shape of the leaves.

Metal Sculpture

Materials: Small, thin pieces of wire, 1 4 x 4" block of wood for stand, glue gun.

Method: Demonstrate how to move and create shapes with the wire. Make sure each client has an idea of what they might make. Emphasize that this can be very abstract. Have them work with a few pieces and encourage them to retry their piece until it feels complete. Glue to the block of wood.

Shoe Away!

Materials: Shoe inserts, old soles, cardboard cutouts of various sizes of shoes, large sheet of construction paper – any color, markers, crayons, or colored pencils.

Method: Talk about walking in someone else's shoes! Whose shoes would they like to walk in? A ballerina? A runner? Explain that they will have some examples of soles of shoes and 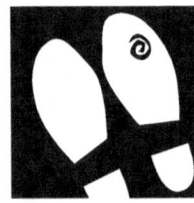 they can pick as many or as few as they wish. They will place these on the paper and glue them down. After putting enough shoes on the page, they can add color to the spaces outside the soles. It might even be interesting to make very small shoes…

<u>Vegetable Stamps</u>

Materials: potatoes, carrots, or other piece of vegetable that can be cut in half and used to stamp on paper, thick tempera paint, large sheet of heavy duty paper, cardboard.

Method: Discuss vegetables and how when halved, they can still be identified. Cut a potato in half. Pass it around. Talk about the smell, the feel. Do the same with a large carrot. Then ask clients to take one piece of vegetable and experiment by dipping it into thick paint and printing it on the paper. When they paint is dry, they will be able to feel the outline of the vegetable.

Stepping Stones

Materials: Several bags of small smooth stones (available at Dollar Store for pennies), glue gun, large round cement block or piece of linoleum.

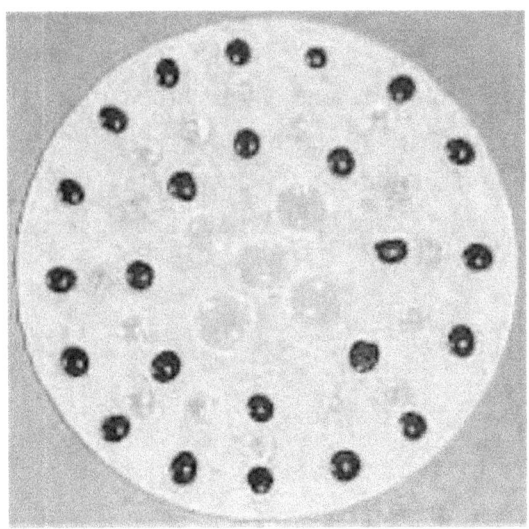

Method: Glue stones onto the entire block of cement or linoleum. Have clients stand on one completed stepping stone so they understand how it might feel if they missed a spot! Talk about the process! The stones can be closer together or far apart as pictured here.

Building a Stool

Materials: A 12" or larger round piece of wood, three wooden 3x3 16" dowels, carpenter's glue, three long screws, screwdriver, 0000 sandpaper, optional paint, varnish.

Method: 1 completed stool. Prepare in advance a partial hole for the screws to be inserted from the top of the stool. Talk about stability and that the stool needs three legs the same size. Have each one insert a screw into the to down and into one of the legs. Use the screwdriver to attach it. (First place Carpenter's glue on the top of the leg that will attach under the seat.) Repeat with each leg. Allow to dry. Sandpaper any rough edges. Check out for stability of stool. Wipe off and paint, if so desired. When paint is finished, can add coat of shellac. These sell from the Amish store online for $32.50. You can probably make it for less than $10!

Flowered Hands

Materials:
finger paint
or other
thick paint,
felt or
construction
paper
leaves and
stems; 8 x
11" poster
board or
thick paper, glue.

Method: Place hand in wet paint and place on the sheet of paper. When dry, feel where the hand is and add stem and leaves. Talk about the kinds of smells flowers have. Pass out some real flowers for them to smell and identify which ones they prefer.

Big Origami

Materials: Large 10 x 10 sheets of origami paper. Following are several shapes to make using the paper.

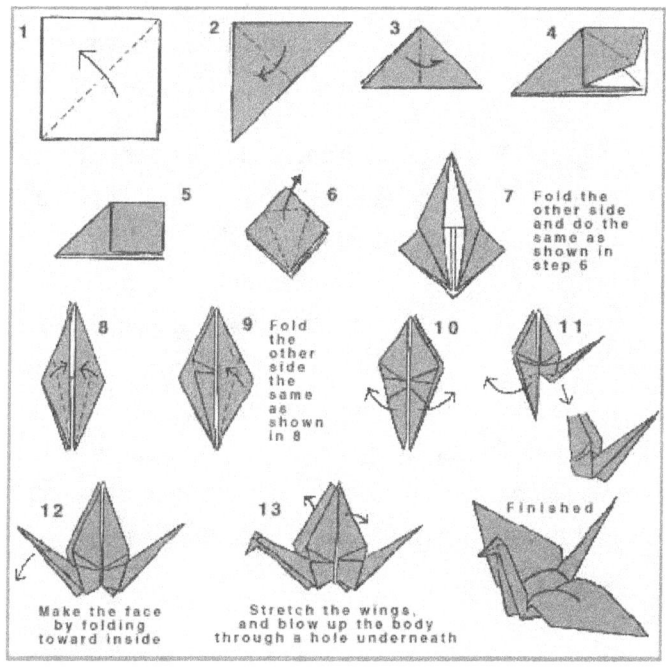

Method: http://www.instructables.com/id/How-to-make-a-Paper-Crane/?skipPro=true&sourcea=comment&newComment=true#POST

Mud Play

Materials: About one quart of mud for each client, (optional: make your own mud – add water to dirt, keep consistency thick). 10x10" or any size sturdy cardboard or thin plywood, water basin with soap, water basin with no soup, towels.

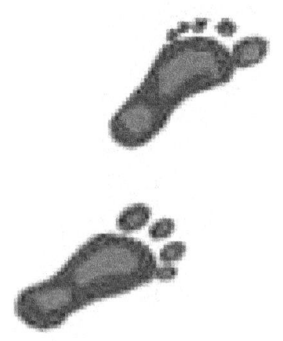

Method: Did you ever play in the mud? What is mud? Have clients touch the mud or make a bit of their own. When the discussion slows down, ask each client to place his/her bare foot in the mud and then place on the cardboard or wood. Clients may decide to do either or both of their feet. Immerse feet in soapy water, rinse in clean basin and dry. A great reminder of childhood memories might erupt….

Straw Bridges

Materials: 50 straws or less for each person, masking tape, a sheet of cardboard or other sturdy base, blunt edged scissors.

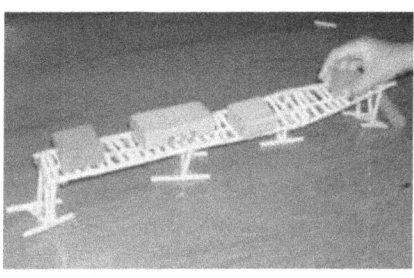

Method: Begin by talking about bridges. What are bridges? What kinds of bridges do they believe they have been on? Why do we have bridges? What do they connect? Allow clients to work solo or with a partner, if they so desire. Encourage each to build a bridge that will hold a book. Have each one hold the book and see its weight. When completed have each one try to see if their bridge is sturdy enough to hold the book. Are there such things as mental bridges? What do we have to know to do something? What are some of their experiences?

Food Art

Materials: cooked sticky rice, almonds, cinnamon, sweetener, raisins, sesame seeds, various types of candies, plate.

Method: Have you ever eaten sticky rice? What might it taste like to you? Each person can taste a spoonful of it. Do you  like it? Would you like to change the taste? Would it be better sweet? What can we add to make it sweeter? Give each client a bowl of sticky rice (make sure hands are washed beforehand). They will each be able to add sweetener, cinnamon, and/or vanilla. Have them mix the ingredients. Add almonds, raisins or other candies to the mixture. Form a ball. When finished, add details on the outside. Eat and enjoy!

<u>Pizza</u>

Materials: 1 (.25 ounce) package active dry yeast, 1 teaspoon white sugar, 1 cup warm water (110°F/45°C), 2-1/2 cups bread flour, 2 tablespoons olive oil, 1 teaspoon salt, toppings.

Method: Preheat oven to 450°F (230°C). In a medium bowl, dissolve yeast and sugar in warm water. Let stand until creamy, about 10 minutes.

Stir in flour, salt, and oil. Beat until smooth. Let rest for 5 minutes. Turn dough out onto a lightly floured surface and pat or roll into a round. Transfer crust to a lightly greased pizza pan or baker's peel dusted with cornmeal. Spread with desired toppings and bake in preheated oven for 15 to 20 minutes, or until golden brown. Let baked pizza cool for 5 minutes before serving.

Apple Carving

Materials: apple, paring knife.

Method: Talk about times when people carve vegetables, such as pumpkins, etc. Ask clients what they could do with an apple. Distribute a plastic knife to each one. Summarize what they are doing and why. How does it feel to carve? Can we carve out own lives out? Topic for discussion….

Dried Apple Rings

Materials: 1 apple, plastic knife, string.

Method: Wash apple, cut into thin slices, stringing each piece onto the string. Hang up until dry. Talk about the smell. What does it evoke? Eat finished product or make into a wreath to hang for fragrance.

Glass Collage

Materials: glass pieces (buy prepared pieces that aren't sharp), thin plywood or thick cardboard pieces, paint, brushes, glue gun.

Method: Have clients feel the glass pieces of varying sizes. They will lay them down on the plywood or cardboard. Have them decide when they are finished. Hot glue the pieces to the frame.

Puppets on a TP Roll

Materials: Toilet paper roll, newspaper cut into strips or town, liquid starch, large bowl, acrylic paint, brush, material, found objects for eyes, mouth; yarn for hair, masking tape.

Method: Ball up 1 to 2 sheets of newspaper and secure with masking tape to form the head. Tape the roll to a small

square of poster board or cardboard. Dip strips of newspaper into starch and cover head until desired size. Allow to dry 36 hours. Paint desired color of head. (I ask my clients if they would like to have the same color as they are or another color.) Hot glue the eyes, mouth and nose on. Hot glue 5-6" pieces of yarn on the head for hair. The last phase is the outfit. Provide clients with precut pattern piece for the puppet dress. Depending upon the material, clients can sew the inside with a large blunt needle and yarn (good if the material is felt or a loose weave).

(www.weefolkart.com).

Cardboard Bird

Materials: TP roll, scissors, glue gun, pencil

Method: Cut the tp roll into thirds. One third will be the head; one third the body, and the other third can be opened up to create a tail, wing, and beak. Use the illustration below to guide you. It might be a good idea to put precut wings into one container. Precut tails and beaks into another container. Blind clients can then pull out the size of the ones they need.

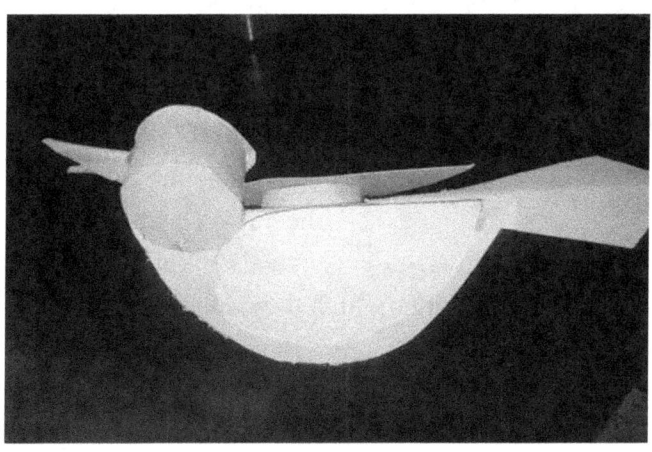

Mandala for the Blind

Materials: White glue, Large circle cut out of a sheet of poster paper, masking tape, markers, small squares of colored construction paper.

Method: Create a prototype for the client to feel. Take the glue and create a circular shape, adding shape and texture as you go around the inside, until arriving at the center of the sheet. Allow the glue to dry. Color in the between spaces with small and/or large markers. Clients can also use small squares of construction paper which they adhere to the circle until it is all filled in. I usually tape the circle down.

Discuss the history of the mandala – ancient shape – circular – stars, moon, sun, flowers, trunks of trees – shapes of the inside of our eyes, circles are everywhere. Is life cyclical?

<u>Woodworking Ideas</u>

Materials: Eight 18" x 10" thin plywood (max 1/2" thick), carpenter's glue, hammer, short nails, one large thin backing (check building store for inexpensive backing materials – light weight), 0000 sandpaper, varnish.

Method: Demonstrate a model of a small bookshelf for the clients. Tell them they can make up to four shelves with the material. They will set them up one by one, gluing and nailing each to a side piece. After all shelves are nailed to a side, the back is tacked on. Sand rough edges until smooth. Varnish with a coat of shellac.

Metal Wind Chimes

Materials: 1" paint brush, primer for wood stain, wood stain, clear coat polyurethane, mineral spirits, 00 steel wood, 5 ft. length of 3/4 inch copper tubing, cut into irregular lengths (about 5), scrap piece of 1x10 planking, approximately 6 ft of decorative chain, cut into six equal pieces, a small piece of golden craft wire, five small sized "I" screws, three small brass hooks, one heavy key ring.

Method: If needed, use the steel wool to sand pieces until smooth, clean with mineral spirits, coat with primer and then wood stain. When dry, coat with polyurethane. Assembly: space the eye bolts, all dependent upon the size of the chime's clapper – one for each tube, and one right in the center for the clapper chain. Once you've set the eye bolts (these'll be to hold the actual chime tubes), on the top side you'll need to secure the small hooks, these will attach the chain to the large key ring.

On the clapper, drill a small hole through the middle and use a short piece of the golden craft wire to attach the chain to the top and bottom. The upper chain attaches to the top and the bottom chain (which should extend well below the longest tube) goes to the weight.

After the placement of the eye bolts and the small hooks, at whichever lengths you prefer, cut and bend some of the links in order to attach the chimes to the top, and from the top to the key ring, not to mention the clapper to the top and the down weight to the clapper,

Now all you have to do is attach all these parts to the top, and you're ready to chime! (thanks to the website below for the detailed instructions.)

http://www.instructables. com/id/Copper-tubing- wind-chime/

Button Collage

Materials: Buttons of every shape, texture, and size. Tacky glue, frame (can be cardboard or ver light plywood).

Method: Prepare frame for glue. Spread glue over a small area and begin attaching buttons. Continue until until the entire area is covered and allow to dry.

Soap Carving

Materials: 1 bar Ivory soap for each client, plastic knives, wide plastic bowl in which to place materials, any other sculpting tools available to you.

Method: Pass out several small sculptures and have clients talk about what it feels like. Tell them that the soap they will be carving is very easy to carve and that they will be using materials that also are quite safe. Placing a bar of soap in each plastic bowl (can get inexpensive ones at dollar stores or Goodwill), allow them to work the soap with the plastic knives and other tools.

Orange Potpourri

Materials: fresh orange, box of whole cloves, yarn.

Method: Pass around a model of the orange potpourri. Have clients feel all around the orange. and comment on the smell. Stick cloves into the orange until the orange is completely covered. Wrap the yarn around the orange twice and bring both ends up to tie and hang where desired.

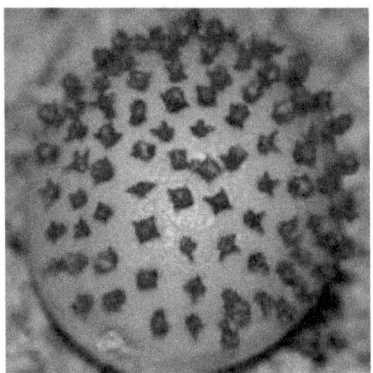

Making an Apron

Materials: One 18"x18" square of felt any color, one 2" wide ribbon approximately 40" long, scissors.

Method: Cut 16 one inch slits in the top of the piece of felt. Weave the ribbon in and out of the slits and tie on! Simple, easy, and very rewarding to have made something! You can also glue on decorative fronts, cutting simple shapes out of other pieces of felt (for the sighted, different colors). You can also glue on pom poms to make it decorative or cut out stars, hearts, or other shapes to glue on the front.

No Sew Fleece Blanket

Materials: 3 yards of polar fleece, scissors.

Method: Be sure all sides are straight. (To figure this out, fold like a triangle and any pieces that aren't exactly flush can be trimmed.) With the scissors, cut 1½" every two fingers' width. Each cut should be about the same length. Complete all edges.

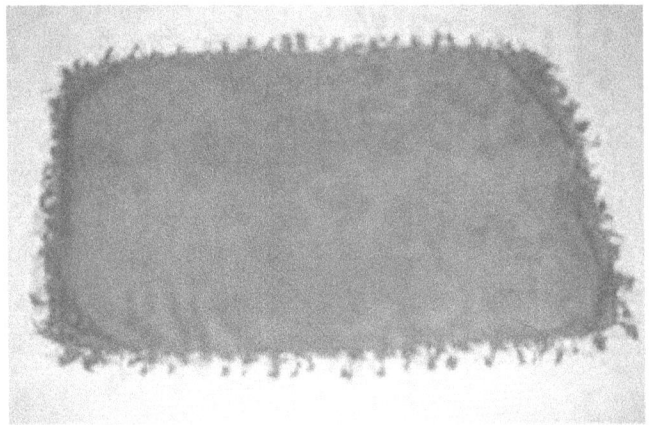

Paper Tissue or Kleenex Flowers

Materials: Six to eight 5" or larger squares of tissue paper, one pipe cleaner for each flower, scissors.

Method: Stack the squares. Fold over one end and fold back the other way, in an accordion style. When completely

folded, find the middle and make a notch in it with the scissors. Wrap the end of a pipe cleaner around this center and twist until the end has disappeared. Finish the edges. (You can cut points or round the edges.) Gently pull each layer of tissue towards the middle until all the layers are pulled. You have a beautiful flower and can use all one color tissue or you can mix it up.

Felt Garden

Materials: 12"x20" or thereabouts piece of heavy felt (like carpet pads). 9 starter plants. Scissors. Soil. Shredded paper. Industrial-type stapler.

Method: Create a horizontal pocket and staple so that the pocket does not rip. Do 2 or 3 on the horizontal edge. With a large needle and thread sew compartments down each strip.

In each pocket deposit some soil and a starter plant and cover with shredded paper. Water well. Hang and enjoy!

Bottle Cap Art

Materials: Cleaned, nonsharp bottle caps. You can paint these by immersing in acrylic or other permanent paints, but not necessary. Thin plywood cutout of fish or other simple object. Carpenter's glue (I usually go back over the work and make sure it is thoroughly glued down using hot glue). Paints, brushes, cleaning materials, aprons to protect your clothing!

Method: Feel the shape of the plywood and decide where the bottle caps will go. Pour enough glue to make sure the caps will stand on end or at an angle. Take your time. When completed, the parts of the cutout not covered with caps may be painted.

Notable Quotes

I don't much like clay. Not at all. And I don't want to use it today or ever.

My therapy hat is on. I see that they are scared. They don't want to touch something of whose origin they are not sure. They haven't learned to trust me yet. I relax and realize that I can figure out a way to do art with them even if it kills me. Not really kills me but totally devastates me and cause me to not pass practicum! I soon become more able to interpret even their smallest remarks... and when I am scared, I can get angry. I can get obstinate. I can go into my cave and you will not move me.

Let's just talk. I don't want to draw today. Can't we just have a discussion?

We're tired. We expend a lot more energy than one would think in finding out where we are going, how to avoid others, and, frankly, we have things we need to talk about today. We trust you enough to meet our needs. Talking and listening might work today.

You've given us choices before so we feel good about asking you for this today. I have learned that I can trust this group and talking helps me a lot. I like to talk about our art.

Yeah.

I'm in pain. I've led a long life filled with pain.
You ask me what I want. What do I want? Not to
be blind! Or to be dead. I did this to myself. And
I am numb to the world.

Yeah.

I'll do what you ask. But I am a robot and feel
nothing. I won't allow myself to feel.

Others just ask how I am and go on to the next
person. It really doesn't matter, does it?

Yeah, I remember seeing. I remember colors. I miss 'em.

You have made me comfortable enough to confide in you. Yes, some awful person threw acid in my face. In fact, that awful person was my father. I hated him. And now he is dead. I am glad. But I do remember the colors. I liked red. Yes, I did.

Chile', those colors are still in my head. I wish I could see them. You have helped me have hope. I want to see with my art.

Don't think you're all that. You're not. We've had a lot of art therapists and teachers here. They always leave.

When people called me retarded, I felt so bad inside. I wanted to shout at them, to hit them. They laughed in my face. I was so hurt. I can think. I can talk. I am not retarded!

Funny how I haven't said that before to anyone. I guess I am feeling pretty comfortable here. But guess what? You will go and someone else will take your place. Maybe that's what is making me mad today. I am mad because I don't want to lose everyone I care about.

Let's play a joke on 'em. I don't get to laugh often.

Enough of this serious business. Can't we just have fun? It's hard enough to be blind. I try my utmost to maintain a measure of decorum. You would never guess I am depressed and lonely.

I don't like where I live. No one else is blind there, so they don't understand my social circle. That's a joke, don't you get it?

My mother won't even let me see her. She says I am dangerous and she is too old to be careful. So she is in California and I am here. I am over 50 yrs. old and I must make the best of life.

I'll miss you, chile'. God bless you.

Lord knows you've listened to me belly ache about my sister. How she bosses me around. It felt good to let it out. In a safe place. Where someone cared. I know you cared, Lola. I cared, too.

Remember when I scared you. You must've thought I was dead or asleep, but I jumped at you. You must've jumped ten feet. It was so funny. Everyone laughed.

I wouldn't play with just anyone like that. Nope, you are special, girl, and I like the way you talk to me and make me feel special. I will remember you always.

My Art

The following pages are dedicated to Robert Morrissey, one of the most wonderful art therapists and mentors I've ever known. He insisted I do art and it scared me at first. But then it started helping me just as it was helping my clients… thanks for the gift, Bob!

See, Mama? I can draw. I'm not the best in my class, but I'm ok!

An exercise in fantasy.

Foreshortening took me forever to get.

One of my favorite pieces. So delicate and sweet.

Learning to draw required learning the structure of bones, tendons, and much more.

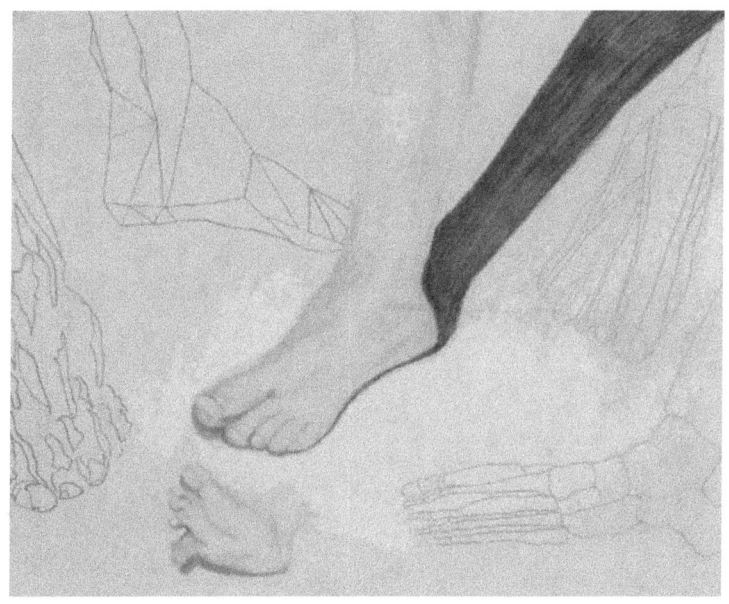

Drawing your own feet looking down is not easy.

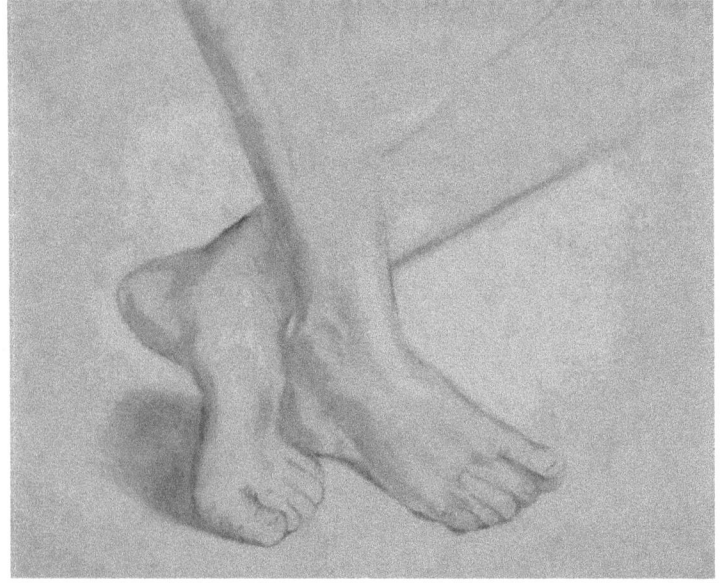

Whoa! The teacher liked this one. Studying the planes on the face surely made me aware of my age!

Working with homeless people allowed me to introduce them to computer generated art.

Collage is great for anyone – having sight made me very grateful and thankful. I realized that my three years in art therapy school was filled with memories, pain, and survival. Funny that this collage was about my family when I was growing up....

I learned a lot during my three years, especially professionalism. May some of it keep rubbing off on me! Next are the three years of our program summarized in cake art!

My final project for Christine Turner, the Dean of the Art Therapy Program. Many thanks to Laura Fitzgibbon, who arranged for me to make this cake and the owner would NOT allow me to pay for ingredients. Beaverton Town Bakery, thank you!

Although not my favorite piece, this one received the best grade of all, so I leave it to the last, reminding everyone that with focus and motivation, we can all be artists!

For more information on how to create a therapeutic relationship with blind individuals, please feel free to email Lola: masabitherapist@gmail.com.

 **If you have additional information you would like to add to this work in process, please contact Lola at the same address above. We are all in this together, so let's work together, no matter what part of the world in which we live.**

These directives do not have to be just for blind clients, they are good for all clients – it's just easier with seeing clients!

Peace and many blessings,

Lola

www.ingramcontent.com/pod-product-compliance
Lightning Source LLC
Chambersburg PA
CBHW070013300526
45794CB00001B/300